THE BEAUTIFUL
HORSE

This is a Parragon Publishing Book
First published in 2007

Parragon Publishing
Queen Street House
4 Queen Street
Bath BA1 1HE, UK

Designed, produced, and packaged by Stonecastle Graphics Limited

Photography © Bob Langrish
Text taken from *Spirit of the Horse* by Nicola Jane Swinney
Designed by Sue Pressley and Paul Turner

ISBN 978-1-4054-8053-6

Printed in China

Page 1: The Morgan is the oldest of all the American breeds. It is a small compact horse with a charming nature and has been an important influence on many modern American breeds.

Pages 2 and 3: Romantics may insist that the Mustang is untameable, but this is not so—it is a tough little horse, but quite biddable, and it often forms strong bonds with humans.

Page 4: The Friesian is a compact, beguiling breed with spectacular paces and an endearing temperament.

Page 5: Both beautiful and fearless, the Andalucian was prized as a warhorse.

Author's note: The term "grey" is used throughout this book to describe a white or gray colored horse.

THE BEAUTIFUL
HORSE

Bob Langrish

Nicola Jane Swinney

p

The horse has been an integral part of our lives for thousands of years, and it is all too easy to forget that it is, essentially, a wild animal.

Throughout history we have radically changed the lives of our horses to suit our own purposes. But despite centuries of domestication, horses still retain their independent character and it is a joy and a privilege to observe their natural behavior—to watch them frolic and play, and kick up their heels with the sheer exuberance of living.

In this book you will find no images of horses being ridden nor in harness, just exquisite pictures of this most beautiful animal as nature intended it to be—a free spirit.

THE HORSE

We are so accustomed to its apparent domesticity—the determined race horses, the athletic show jumpers, and adored children's ponies—that when we see the horse in a more natural environment, free from the trappings of the human world, it can be a revelation. We forget that the horse is part of our lives due to its co-operative nature, not because of our domination of it.

Few other animal species have lived so close to humans, and captivated us for so long. From its early domestication, the horse has gone with us unquestioningly to war—and often perished—has been for a time our foremost mode of transport, and is now our companion in competition and leisure. Its destiny has always been linked with that of mankind, and happily a few areas of our planet still remain populated by wild horses. Where Darwin's law of "survival of the fittest" rules, the horse will continue to evolve, to thrive, and to benefit us for years to come.

THE NATURE OF THE HORSE

Naturally gregarious, horses are herd animals. Any horse owner will know that horses turned out together in a field are likely to form a "pecking order," or hierarchy, and will, for the most part, remain together as a group, even if they are of quite different types and breeds. In the wild, horses instinctively form herds, usually comprising several family groups which include a stallion and perhaps five or six mares and their offspring. As a herd they will sleep, play, and feed while constantly being alert to potential danger.

Although during the mating season the stallions within the groups will fight for dominance over the breeding females, the herd is usually controlled by the older mares, who will keep in check any high spirits among the younger members of the herd, particularly the colts. While domesticated stallions are generally perceived as more dominant and unpredictable than mares, the "matriarchs" of wild herds can be equally aggressive and far from submissive.

Safety for the wild horse is dependent upon a combination of excellent physical and sensory attributes—explosive speed and stamina to outrun any predator, as well as superb vision and hearing to detect the slightest threat. For survival in the wild, the horse depends on the "fight or flight" response.

It has strong, protruding teeth which can used as a "weapon" against another horse during a fight for supremacy.

From a standing start, a horse can reach a top sprint speed of forty-five miles per hour in three or four seconds. Its large eyes, set either side of the head, have almost all-round vision, and its mobile ears, which can rotate almost through three hundred and sixty degrees, act like radar scanners.

There is safety in numbers and a predator is likely to be confused by a group of animals galloping around. Here again, Darwin's theory of "survival of the fittest" comes into play: if a predator does manage to separate an individual from the herd, it is most likely to be old and weak or sickly, leaving the strongest, healthiest members to survive and thrive. The herd's social structure, in which the co-operation of the group is combined with vigilance, helps to preserve the safety of the individual. It also allows herd members to feed, play, and rest in comparative security.

THE EVOLUTION OF THE HORSE

The evolution of the horse is one of the best charted and most famous in all of science. The early Eohippus or "Dawn Horse" was no bigger than a fox. Over millions of years it adapted to suit its environment until it evolved into a number of small equine species which inhabited what is now the North American continent fifteen million years ago.

Hunted for its meat by both man and other predators, the horse population declined to extinction in the isolated continent and no horses inhabited the Americas for over eight thousand years. Then, in the fifteenth century, the arrival of the Spanish conquistadors with their beautiful and powerful steeds changed equine evolution beyond recognition.

Since then, man has appreciated the essential qualities of the horse—its amenable temperament and willingness to please, its physical strength, and its tremendous speed and agility—and through selective breeding has developed these specific characteristics to create the many varied breeds we know today. Living alongside man as servant and companion, the horse is at once compliant and brave, honest and hard-working, but perhaps it would pay us to remember that underneath the domesticated animal, it remains essentially the same wild horse that evolved to roam the open plains.

Page 7: The beautiful Arab breed played an important role in the development of the highly prized English Thoroughbred.

Previous pages: With its tiny curved ears, large liquid eyes, extravagantly dished (concave) face, and luxurious mane and tail, the Arab is the horse of dreams. It is undeniably beautiful and is the purest, and possibly the oldest, of all the breeds.

Left and following pages: One of the most notable differences between the Arab and other breeds is the number of its vertebrae: all other equine breeds have eighteen ribs, six lumbar vertebrae, and eighteen tail bones; the Arab has seventeen ribs, five lumbar vertebrae, and sixteen tail bones. It has another unique feature known as the *mitbah*, which refers to the angle at which the head meets the neck. The Arab's small head with its tapering muzzle (its muzzle should fit into a half-cupped hand) is set high on its fine muscular neck. This results in an arching curve that allows the head to be incredibly mobile and to turn freely in almost any direction. Also unique to the breed is the *jibbah*, a shield-shaped bulge extending between the Arab's huge, wide-set eyes, upward to a point between the ears and down across the top third of the nasal bone.

Above: As much as it is prized for its beauty, the Arab is revered for its speed and stamina, as well as its athleticism. Its action is a joy to behold—it moves freely and lightly, as though on springs—as it appears to float across the ground. The long silky mane and tail, which is carried exceptionally high, contribute to the horse's enchanting appearance.

Left: The Arab is not a big horse, rarely exceeding about 15 hands in height. The grey color—which, as with all breeds, lightens with age—adds to its fairy-tale charm, but all solid colors, except palomino, are seen. Its coat is fine and silky, so the veining can be seen beneath, and has a high sheen, particularly in the chestnut and bright bay.

Left and above: Throughout history, the most common Arab colors were grey, chestnut, brown, or bay. Black was not a popular color as it absorbs heat, and a desert horse would not be as thermally efficient with a black coat. Diligent breeders did their best to eliminate the color from their prized bloodlines but today most Arabs no longer live in the desert and black horses are becoming increasingly popular.

Left and following pages: The Arab's elegant neck sweeps gracefully to rounded withers and strong, sloping shoulders, while its short back, with its high croup, is notably concave. A broad, deep chest, encasing exceptionally strong lungs, gives the breed an ability to work unfailingly for great lengths of time, making them ideal for the sport of endurance riding. The Arab's bone is said to be denser than that of other breeds and its clean, hard legs appear deceptively delicate. The breed is also noted for its good, sound feet which are almost perfect in shape.

Left: This beautiful ancient breed is thought to date as far back as 3000BC and it has strongly influenced many of today's more modern breeds of horse. The Bedouin tribes of the Arab deserts zealously protected and maintained the Arab breed, striving to keep it pure. Any mixture of foreign blood from the mountains or the cities surrounding the desert was strictly forbidden. The Bedouins' highly selective breeding policies shaped the magnificent horse we see today, and which—through centuries of care and commitment—remains highly prized.

Right: Because of the harsh desert conditions in which it was originally found, the Arab would work alongside its nomadic masters—sharing food and water, and often even accommodation. As a result, the breed has developed distinctly high intelligence and a close affinity with man.

Left: Throughout history the Arab has been highly prized as an instrument of war. The mare was deemed best for forays into enemy territory as she would not whinny to the enemy's horses, warning the tribe of the attackers' approach. These wonderful war mares exhibited great courage in battle, taking charges and spear attacks undauntedly. Speed and endurance—for which the Arab is still famous today— were vital, as the raids were often carried out far from the tribe's own camp. The Arab mare was thus beyond price. Possessing both speed and stamina, these remarkable horses were coveted by all who encountered them.

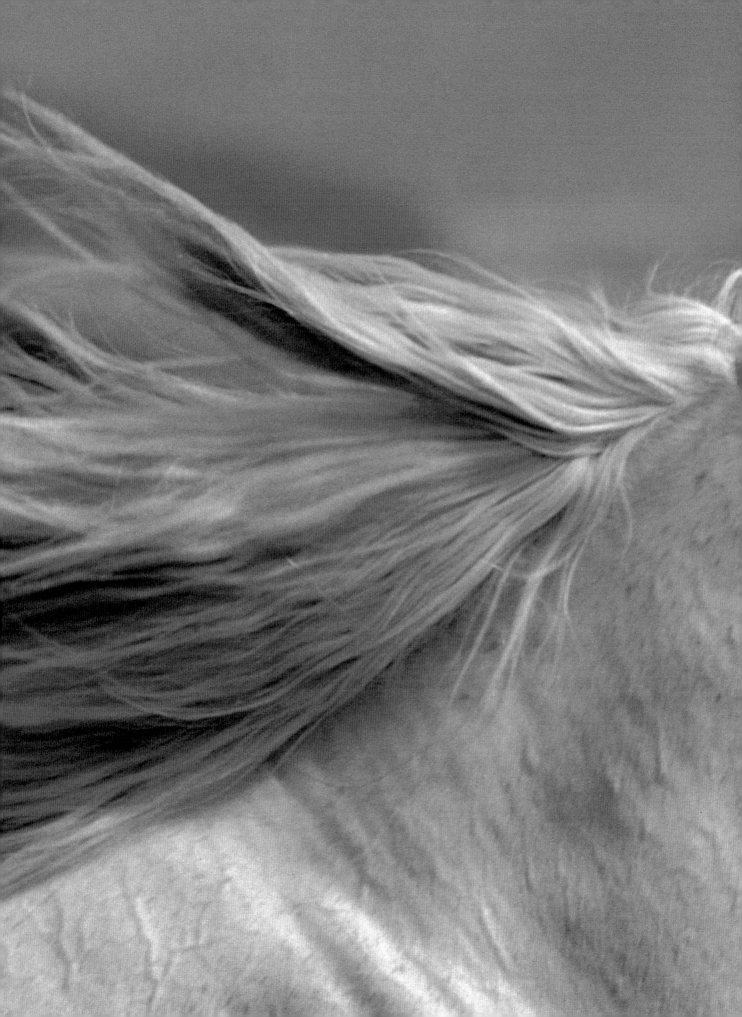

Previous pages and left: It would be impossible to overestimate quite how influential the early Arab horses were in the development of modern breeds around the world. Highly regarded by the military, the breed became increasingly well-known and to own such an impressive horse carried enormous prestige—as breeding from this marvelous creature would improve local stock beyond measure.

Previous pages: The origins of the pure-bred Iberian horse can be traced back to the eighth century and it has played a major role in the development of modern horse breeds.

Above and right: The Spanish Andalucian (above) and its Portuguese cousin the Lusitano (right) still retain the distinct characteristics of the Iberian breed which was renowned for its flamboyant high-stepping gait and extreme agility. Prized as an outstanding cavalry horse from the time of the ancient Greeks, the breed's athletic ability and extravagant action has been instrumental in establishing the art of horsemanship as we now know it today.

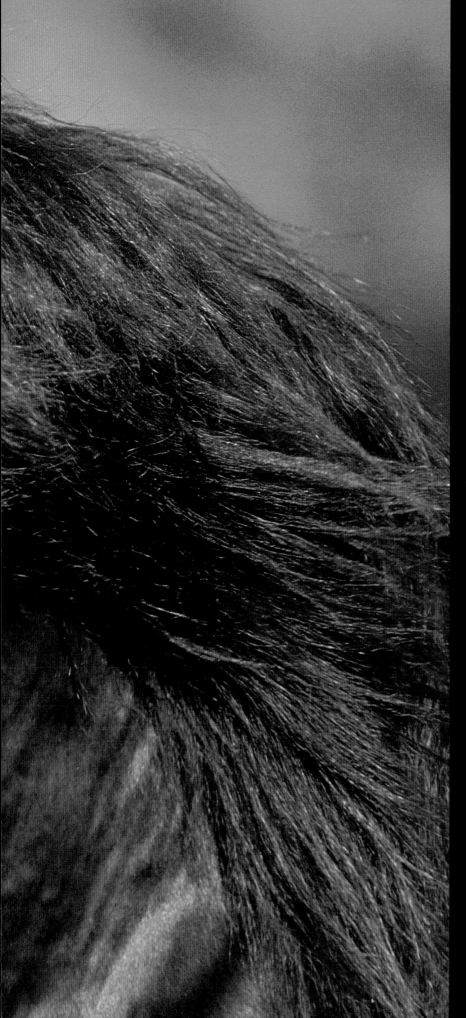

Left: The Iberian horse's beauty and tremendous presence are very striking. Most Andalucians are typically grey in color, although bay, roan, and black are also seen. A compact and short-coupled horse, it stands about 15.2hh, with a sloping croup (hindquarters) and low-set tail. It is undoubtedly intelligent and its noble profile is convex—rather than concave like that of the Arab—and somewhat hawk-like, with a broad forehead. The Andalucian's classically beautiful head is instantly identifiable.

Following pages: The Andalucian has a notably high degree of flexion in the hindlegs, which means it moves naturally in collection—and this agility has played a vital part in the Spanish pure-bred's influence on other breeds. As well as being bred as a warhorse, the Iberian breed was developed for working the lithe black bulls destined for the Spanish bull-ring and it is still used to fight in Spain's traditional arenas to this day. It is not built for galloping, but is incredibly supple and quick on its feet. However, for all its fiery presence, the breed is gentle and docile.

Above and right: Similar in many ways to its Spanish cousin, it is thought that the Lusitano was developed in Portugal by breeding the Andalucian with more Arab blood. At a maximum height of 16hh, this compact breed is renowned for its courage and is both intelligent and quick to learn. Possessing considerable athletic ability and impressive bravery, the Lusitano has been highly prized throughout history as a cavalry mount. Its speed, elevated action, and natural athleticism are clearly demonstrated in the Portuguese bull-ring where the bull-fight is conducted entirely on horseback. Fast, agile, and responsive, the Lusitano is capable of being highly schooled to perform complex dressage movements.

Previous pages: The Lusitano has a Roman nose and wide forehead with large kind eyes, and neat curving ears. It has a short, thick neck which connects with powerful and quite upright shoulders, and a broad chest with plenty of heart room. The breed has a short, compact back with well-sprung ribs, muscular quarters, and long, strong powerful legs. And, typical of the pure-bred Spanish horse, the Lusitano possesses the same abundant, rippling mane and tail as the Andalucian.

Right and following pages: The color of the Lusitano is predominantly grey, although it can also be black, bay, or chestnut. Buckskin and an unusual, striking mulberry shade are also occasionally seen.

Left: Almost every European horse breed possesses at least a trace of Arab blood and there is no greater example of this than the English Thoroughbred. Revered throughout the world for its turn of hoof, its stamina, and its beauty, this breed is a direct descendant of the Arab. The Thoroughbred has been developed as a powerful racing machine—eleven hundred pounds of bone and muscle capable of sprinting at speeds of more than forty-five miles per hour. It is bred to race and its strength of character gives it a potent determination to win.

Right: Today's racehorse is a creature of great beauty and presence, which it owes to its Arab inheritance. Standing at around 16hh, it has a fine, lean head with a straight profile—unlike its concave-faced ancestors—with big, expressive eyes, and large nostrils.

Previous pages and above: Throughout history man has desired better, faster, and stronger horses, so the monarchy and nobility (who were the principal patrons and participants in the sport of racing) longed to find a breed designed primarily for speed. One vital element was missing from the early racehorses—Arab blood. With the introduction in the late eighteenth century of three foundation stallions, The Byerley Turk, The Darley Arabian, and The Godolphin Arabian, the English Thoroughbred was born.

Right: The Darley Arabian sired Flying Childers, who in turn sired superb racing stock. His great-great-nephew, Eclipse, was perhaps the most famous racehorse of all time. He was unbeaten in all eighteen of his races and went on to sire an estimated three hundred winners. Many of today's successful racehorses can be traced back to this foundation stock.

Following pages: Thoroughbreds begin their training at two years old. After their racing careers, they may be retired to

Left: The Thoroughbred has, over the centuries, been used to refine and improve other stock. Crossed with native Irish ponies the Thoroughbred produced a lighter draft horse with speed and character which was further refined with blood from the ubiquitous Spanish horse. The Irish Draft is a superb sports horse. Big and strong—stallions can stand 17hh tall—it has a comparatively small, intelligent head, which is perhaps due to the influence of the Connemara pony in early stock. The best Irish Drafts have strong sound legs and a straight, free action; they possess excellent shoulders and are natural jumpers. They are much in demand as show jumpers and hunters—across country, they are hard to beat. The Irish hunter is said to have an uncanny ability when jumping to "find an extra leg"—and thus get itself, and its rider, out of trouble. The addition of Thoroughbred blood gives them added quality and speed.

Above: The Friesian breed owes much to the Spanish Andalucian. "Cold blooded"—as opposed to the "hot blooded" Thoroughbred or Arab—it is a stocky draft horse. Acknowledged by the Romans as being a superlative work animal, and highly valued as a knight's charger, the breed is thought to date back as far as 1000BC. Although not a big horse, it has tremendous bearing and an impressive high-stepping action. As well as being tough and hardy, the Friesian has a sweet and biddable nature and makes an excellent harness horse.

Right and following pages: Modern warmbloods are in great demand as sports horses. They are so-called because the breed derives from a mix of "hotblood"—from the Arab or Thoroughbred lines—with "coldblood" from the heavier draft breeds. One of the most successful of all warmblood breeds is the Hanoverian (pictured here and overleaf) which has excelled in both show jumping and dressage, and is in great demand as a competition horse. It is a handsome breed, with an amenable temperament, powerful limbs, and a long, energetic stride.

Left: Thoroughbred blood has also played a part in refining the Holstein. It has, over the years, been developed from a cavalry mount into a talented competition horse and is very much in demand as a hunter, show jumper, eventer, and dressage horse. The modern Holstein is much lighter than earlier examples of the breed, with a finer head and generally more quality.

Above: The Trakehner is one of the most elegant of all warmbloods and the closest to the competition horse ideal, possessing excellent, well-balanced conformation, combined with athletic free paces and stamina. Its long, elegant neck, and well-shaped shoulders echo its Thoroughbred inheritance.

Following pages: The handsome Selle Français, or French Saddle Horse is an extremely versatile and popular horse which excels in a variety of equestrian sports.

Left: The sight of the "dancing white stallions" of the Spanish Riding School of Vienna is unforgettable—the magnificent horses leap and pirouette in their extraordinary "airs above the ground" with unimaginable athleticism and grace. These are the world-famous Lipizzaners, derived largely from the Iberian horse—an ancestry which is acknowledged by the word "Spanish" in the riding school's title. The breed takes its name from the town where it was first bred in 1580, Lipizza (or Lipiça), in what was then part of the Austro-Hungarian Empire. A compact, muscular horse, the Lipizzaner is born dark, sometimes almost black, but as it matures it is almost always grey—lightening to white. Bays are also sometimes seen and one is always resident at the Vienna school. The modern Lipizzaner is based on just six stallions, who have their own distinct characteristics which they pass on to their progeny.

Left: England's best-known heavy horse breed, the Shire, is spectacular; it can stand 18hh or even taller. The Shire descended from the medieval warhorse initially developed to be sufficiently strong to bear a knight in full armor and carrying weighty weapons, and still remain agile enough to carry him into battle. Following centuries of loyal service as a draft animal, the Shire almost became extinct after World War II due to increasing mechanization. But thanks to a number of dedicated breeders, the Shire Horse was saved from extinction and it has since enjoyed a revival. The Shire combines substance with undeniable quality. Its noble head, with its Roman (convex) nose, is long and lean, and its large kind eye is full of intelligence. It has a comparatively long neck for a draft horse and a broad, powerful chest, deep girth, and short back, with well-muscled quarters. Its clean, hard limbs have plenty of bone and abundant long, fine hair—known as feather—around the feet. Shires crossed with Thoroughbreds often make strong and talented show jumpers.

Following pages: Displaying many characteristics of its close relative the Shire, the Clydesdale has a flamboyant, flashy style with a spirited bearing and a high-stepping action that makes it a singularly elegant animal among draft horses. It is a lighter and more elegant breed than the Shire, with noticeably longer legs, a finer, lighter head, longer neck, and a straighter profile. The average height is 16.2hh and it is renowned for its good limbs and hard, enduring feet.

Previous pages: Everyone who has seen a Wild West movie or a rodeo will be familiar with the Mustang. These tough little horses continue to populate areas of North America's great plains, and are thought to have done so for about seven hundred years. The word Mustang derives from the Spanish *mesteña*—meaning a herd of "stray" or "ownerless" horses—and the breed is thought to have evolved from horses brought over by early Spanish explorers. Some of those horses escaped and took up residence in the wild, forming herds. They are notoriously shy and naturally fearful of people, yet like most equines, they can be tamed. They are used as "cow ponies" and their speed and agility when working are renowned.

Right: The Mustang is a small stocky horse standing barely more than 14hh, although height can vary from 13hh up to 16hh. Since its arrival in America, other breeds—such as the Morgan, Friesian, and Thoroughbred—have been added to the mix and occasionally a "throwback" to one of its distinctive Andalucian ancestors appears in the wild herds. Mustangs come in all colors, shapes, and sizes, although they all possess hard feet, sound legs, and a tough constitution. The most common colors are sorrel, or light chestnut, with a flaxen mane and tail, and bay. "Paints"—skewbald or piebald— palomino, and black are also seen.

Previous pages: It is thought that the Native American Indians were the first to tame the wild Mustang and it changed their lives. To the Native Americans, the horse meant status and nobility. It became invaluable in war and when hunting the mighty buffalo. It was also used as currency and it could buy a bride. When a chieftain died, his horses were sacrificed to join him on the "other side." But it wasn't long before the white man began to settle in the newly-discovered continent and cowboys then adopted the Mustang as their mount. The nimble little horse seems to possess an innate "cattle sense" in that it can anticipate what a cow will do next, and this trait secured its place in the cowboy's way of life. Today, this skill can be seen in Western riding competitions, where the Mustang excels.

Above: One theory to explain the origins of the semi-wild ponies on the islands of Assateague, off the east coast of America, and its neighbor Chincoteague, a picturesque Virginian resort, is that the ponies swam ashore from a shipwrecked Spanish galleon. The ponies tend to be small in stature, standing an average of 12hh and most of them are skewbald or piebald, although solid colors do occur.

Right and following pages: An infusion of Arab blood has greatly improved the quality of the Chincoteague ponies, producing highly intelligent and versatile mounts suitable for children. Every July, the ponies are rounded up on Assateague and swum across to Chincoteague, where they are auctioned. Those which remain unsold are swum back to their island the following day.

Opposite: The Paint—formerly known as the Pinto—is designated as a breed only in the United States. Elsewhere "paint" is considered a color rather than a breed. Its original name came from the Spanish word for painted—*pintado*—a very good description. Its color is further defined as Overo or Tobiano. Overo describes a dark coat with splashes of white and is most commonly found in South America. Tobiano is white with large well-defined dark patches, and it is found in North America. The Paint is a compact horse generally standing between 15–16hh.

Left: America's National Show Horse combines the beauty of the Arab with the charisma of the Saddlebred. It is a new breed specifically developed as an athletic horse to exhibit beauty and refinement in the show ring. The breed has an attractive, upright appearance with a long neck, and relatively small head. Large eyes, small ears, fine bone, a high-set flowing tail, together with an elevated action, and natural presence all combine to make the National Show Horse a beautiful sight to behold.

Left: The American Saddlebred has been termed the "peacock of the show ring." It combines spectacular and unique paces with great presence. A practical animal as well as a striking one, the Saddlebred is reminiscent of the English Hackney, with its flashy, high-stepping gait. It makes an excellent harness horse as well as a show-ring star. Bred principally in Kentucky's Blue Grass country, the horse has benefitted from Thoroughbred blood. The Saddlebred is a most handsome horse with striking paces, which in the "five-gaited" Saddlebred include a four-beat slow prancing movement and a full-speed high-stepping "rack."

Following pages: America's most famous breed is probably the Quarter Horse. The name derives from the fact that it was bred to race over a quarter-mile. This name does not derive, as is often mistakenly stated, from the fact that it is a "quarter Thoroughbred." It is, in fact, descended from the early Spanish horses, mixed with Arab and English Thoroughbred blood. The Quarter Horse was bred for speed and is still the fastest of all equine sprinters. It stands a little over 15hh with heavily muscled quarters and hindlegs and powerful forelegs which give it the characteristic burst of speed. This impressive speed, combined with agility and intelligence make it a superb ranch horse. It also possesses an innate "cattle sense." Perhaps this is not surprising, given its Spanish origins—the early Spanish horses were renowned for their prowess in the bull-ring.

Above: The striking and instantly recognizable Appaloosa was developed by the Nez Perce Indian tribe in the lands that became the states of Oregon, Washington, and Idaho, and it takes its name from the Palouse river. Horses brought to America by the Spanish conquistadors included spotted strains and those genes continued to breed through so that the Appaloosa's distinctive markings became as highly prized as their hardiness and willing temperament.

Right: Breeding of the Appaloosa was strictly selective and the modern breed now has five recognizable coat patterns: Leopard, white with dark spots; Snowflake, white spots all over the body but concentrated over the hindquarters; Blanket, where the quarters may be white or spotted; Marble, a mottled pattern over the body; and Frost, white specks on a dark background. As well as its striking coloring, the Appaloosa has other distinctive characteristics including an unusually sparse tail, a white sclera encircling the iris of the eye, and mottled skin around the muzzle. Its hard, sound feet are often vertically striped.

Left: The Rocky Mountain Pony was bred purely for its practicality. Like most American breeds, its origins lie with the early Spanish imports but it has been developed to create a horse for all levels of riders with comfortable smooth paces, pleasing conformation, and amenable temperament. No breed standard has yet been set for the Rocky Mountain. It is a compact animal, standing at 14.2-14.3hh. Although it was primarily developed as a practical, rather than ornamental breed, it is undeniably good looking, possessing a full flaxen mane and tail, together with a coloring which is unusual in other equine breeds.

Left: The Tennessee Walking Horse is named for its gliding, running walk at which it can maintain speeds of up to nine miles per hour. Descended from the Spanish horse, it has three exceptional inherited gaits: the flat walk, the running walk, and a smooth canter.

Above: The Missouri Fox Trotter is one of the least known American breeds. It was originally bred for racing, but its smooth, comfortable action (known as the fox trot), and ability to travel great distances at speed, soon made it a popular choice for riding.

Previous pages: The Peruvian Paso, and the closely related Paso Fino, bear a striking resemblance to their Andalucian cousins. Like the Saddlebred and the Tennessee Walking Horse, these horses have distinctive gaits. The word *"paso"* means "step" in Spanish. The Peruvian Paso was first established in Peru, South America, from horses brought over by a Spanish adventurer. The horse is thought to be one-quarter Andalucian blood and three-quarters Barb. The Barb is an ancient breed which originated from the Barbary Coast of North Africa. It is a tough little horse which has influenced many of the breeds we know today.

Left and right: The Paso Fino is related to the Peruvian Paso and was developed in Puerto Rico. Highly selective breeding over a period of three hundred years has created the Paso's most distinctive feature—the lateral gait for which it is famed. Its forelegs display extravagant, dishing actions, while its powerful hindlegs and lowered quarters drive it forward. There are three inherited gaits: the *paso fino*, a collected, elevated movement; the *paso corto*, an easy traveling pace and the *paso largo*, an extended fast gait which the horse can sustain for some distance, and which is extremely comfortable for its rider. The Paso Fino, like the Peruvian Paso, is not a big horse, usually standing between 14-15hh, but it is hardy and possesses great stamina. It can maintain a steady speed of eleven miles per hour over rough and difficult terrain.

INDEX